About This Book

Out & About Math is the perfect resource to help your students make the connection between the math skills they learn in the classroom and real-life applications. Packed with loads of thematic fun, each activity helps teach national math standards in a developmentally appropriate way. *Out & About Math* contains nine curriculum-based teaching units. Each unit features a different real-life location, such as the playground, the flower shop, and the pet store. The activities within each unit are designed to "pull out" the math that would naturally occur in the featured location. Specific skills are listed at the beginning of each activity, so you'll quickly know which skills are being reinforced. Each unit contains student reproducibles and/or pattern pages used in conjunction with the activities. The *Out & About Math* activities are designed to encourage your students to use higher-level thinking and problem-solving skills with real-life applications.

What Is Real-Life Math?

Traditionally, students have been taught *how* to do math but not *why* they are doing math. In one of its fact sheets on mathematics education, the National Council of Teachers of Mathematics (NCTM) states, "...mathematics must entail the study, understanding, and application of a set of concepts and skills commonly used by real people, in real settings, every day." Math in the real world isn't a row of math problems to solve. Instead, real-world math involves bringing together an array of skills in order to solve daily problems, answer questions, plan tasks, or gather and interpret data. Textbook math often involves contrived, single-step problems to which there is one correct answer. Real-world problems, on the other hand, occur naturally and are often multistep. A person has to decide which procedure or strategy to use to solve a real-life problem. Sometimes there is missing data in a real-world problem that has to be collected in order to solve the problem. Sometimes a real-world problem can have more than one answer, as well as more than one strategy for achieving the answer. Thinking mathematically and then applying this knowledge to everyday situations is very empowering for students. The activities in *Out & About Math* help students develop their mathematical thinking skills as well as an appreciation for math in their everyday lives.

How to Use This Book

Out & About Math is designed to help you meet the needs of your students as well as your needs as a teacher. Each of the nine units is centered around a familiar location. This allows students to recall prior experiences in each location and apply that knowledge to the hands-on activities. Since it's not feasible to take students to each real-life location, the units are designed to bring the locations to the students. A variety of activities—such as center activities, small-group activities, and whole-group activities—are provided in each unit. The pick-and-choose nature of the units allows you to select just the right activities to meet the particular needs of your students. To help you even more, skill lines have been included just below each activity title so that at a glance you can determine the skills addressed in each activity. We've also provided a handy organizer (page 5) listing all the skills covered in the book.

Table of Contents

National Standard	Skill	Craft Store	Pet Store	Bakery	Picnic	Birthday Party	Flower Shop	Playground	Train Shop	Post Office
Number and Operations	adding two-digit numbers without regrouping						●			
	addition									●
	counting				●					
	equality and inequality symbols		●							●
	estimation	●				●		●		●
	even and odd numbers								●	
	fact families					●				
	fractional parts of a set			●						
	fractional parts of a whole	●		●		●				
	making sets		●		●	●			●	
	ordinal numbers									●
	place value to 100s				●		●			
	skip-counting		●						●	
	solving word problems		●			●	●			
	subtraction			●						
Algebra	creating patterns	●	●	●			●			
	extending patterns						●			
	sorting			●						
Measurement	adding bills								●	
	adding coins	●		●						
	bill combinations					●				
	calendar	●								●
	elapsed time								●	
	grouping coins		●							
	linear measurement—nonstandard							●	●	
	linear measurement—standard	●								●
	making change with coins			●						
	selecting and using appropriate tools			●						●
	time to the hour and half hour					●				
	weight									●
Geometry	identifying coordinate points								●	
	identifying plane figures							●		
	identifying solid shapes			●						
	identifying spatial relationships							●		
	sorting shapes			●						
Data Analysis and Probability	bar graph							●		
	completing a chart					●				●
	conducting a survey									●
	displaying and interpreting data					●		●		
	make-a-list strategy		●		●			●		
	picture graph			●						
	possible outcomes				●					
	probability					●				
	tally marks						●			●

WOODEN BEADS   WOODEN BEADS

POM-POMS   POM-POMS

WIGGLE EYES   WIGGLE EYES   CRAFT STICKS

Bead It!
Skill: creating a pattern

"Bead-azzle" your students with this patterned backpack-decoration workshop! In advance, gather a supply of pony beads in six different colors and place each color in a different shallow bowl. For each child, cut a 22-inch length of yarn, tape one end to prevent the yarn from unraveling, and then tie a large knot in the opposite end to secure the beads that will be added later.

Next, tell students that they are at a workshop to make patterned backpack decorations. Divide students into small groups and provide each group with bowls of beads. Give each child a length of yarn. Instruct the student to think of a desired pattern (AB, ABB, ABC), select the corresponding beads, and lay them on his desk. Then direct him to repeat the pattern seven to 20 times, depending on the type of pattern used. Next, have each student thread his beads in order over the taped end of the yarn. Before removing the tape, help him tie a large knot. Have the student slide half of his beads to one yarn end and then slide the remaining half to the opposite end. Demonstrate how to fold the yarn in half and attach the middle section to a backpack zipper as shown. What a crafty idea!

CRAFT SUPPLIES

wiggle eyes	2¢
yarn	10¢
pipe cleaner	3¢
sequin	5¢
button	2¢
craft stick	3¢
glitter	6¢
bead	1¢

Highland Knitters YARN

Making a Creative Purchase
Skill: identifying and adding coins

Spend! Spend! Spend! Children love to spend money, and with this activity they will know which coins to spend! Explain to your little consumers that they need to recognize the coins needed in order to buy craft supplies. Write on the chalkboard the pricing chart shown. Give each student scrap paper, coin manipulatives (pennies, nickels, and dimes), and a pencil. Have each child select one craft item from the list, draw it on her paper, and write the price beside the drawing. Then, using her manipulatives, have her choose the corresponding coins needed to pay for the item. Direct her to draw the coins below the illustration. Have students continue in this manner for three more items. If desired, provide each student with the listed craft supplies after all work is completed and have her design a gift, make it, price it, and use the coins to determine the total price. For further practice with adding money, have each student complete a copy of page 9.

It's a "Mat-ter" of Measurement!
Skill: linear measurement

Show students that measurement is a work of art with this fun activity! Explain to students that matting is a way to frame something. Display and discuss several matted and framed pictures. Tell students that in order to get the correct size mat at a craft store, they must measure each side of their masterpieces. Then provide each student with a 1" x 24" strip of tagboard (a sentence strip that has been cut lengthwise into thirds); a 7" x 7" or a 10" x 4" piece of drawing paper, a pencil, a ruler, scissors, and glue.

Next, have each student measure and then label each side of her paper with its corresponding length. To create the mat, direct her to measure and then cut each sentence strip one inch shorter than the length of the paper's corresponding side. Direct each student to decorate the strips and then glue them on the paper as shown. Then instruct the student to draw a picture on the paper. Have students take their matted pictures home to share with family members. Now that's picture-perfect measurement!

Quilt Making
Skill: identifying fractional parts of a whole

Combine quilt making and a review of fractions with this partner activity. Divide students into pairs. Have students imagine they are making a quilt using squares of paper. Discuss with students that a fraction shows an equal part of a whole. Give each pair one sheet each of blue, red, green, and purple paper. Instruct the pair to make 16 quilting blocks by folding each sheet of paper into fourths and then cutting along the folds to make four equal sections. Ask each pair to create one quilt by laying only red, purple, and green quilting blocks on a work surface. Invite two volunteer pairs to come to the board and write the fractional amounts that each color represents in their quilts. Continue in the same manner with different color combinations. To conclude the activity, have each pair create an original quilt by gluing any number and color combination of quilting blocks on a sheet of white construction paper. Then have the pair write the color name and the corresponding fractional amount of each quilt block on the paper. For further practice with fractions, have each student complete a copy of page 10.

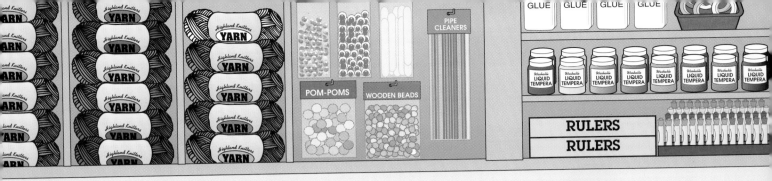

Gift Boxes

Skill: estimating

Improve students' estimation skills with this quick and simple center idea! Ahead of time, gather three different-sized tissue boxes. Label each box with a letter *A* through *C*. Place the boxes, a craft stick, a supply of paper, and a pencil at a center. Tell students to imagine that they are designing gift boxes, but first, they must determine how many craft sticks are needed to cover the sides of their boxes. To use the center, have a student choose a box and write its letter on his paper. Then have the student manipulate the craft stick to estimate how many sticks are needed to cover one of the four sides of the box as shown. Have him write his estimate beside the corresponding letter and then continue in the same manner with each remaining side. Tell the student to add the numbers to get the total estimated number of sticks needed. Have the student continue estimating in the same manner with each remaining box. After every student has had an opportunity to visit the center, display the actual totals for each box. Have students check their guesses for accuracy. Ask several volunteers to share their estimation strategies with the class.

Timely Activities

Skill: completing and interpreting a calendar

Help students make time for fun with this challenging scheduling activity. Provide each student with a copy of page 11. Tell students that they are taking art classes at the local craft store. Challenge students to complete the calendar to determine which days they are available to take new classes. Explain that if there is another activity already scheduled, students cannot schedule a class on that day. Allow time for students to check each other's work and discuss successful strategies for completing the calendar. Students will have this problem solved in no time!

Name_____

Creative Crafts

Read the prices.
Color the coins needed to buy each item.

Attention Customers!
1 Nickel = 5¢

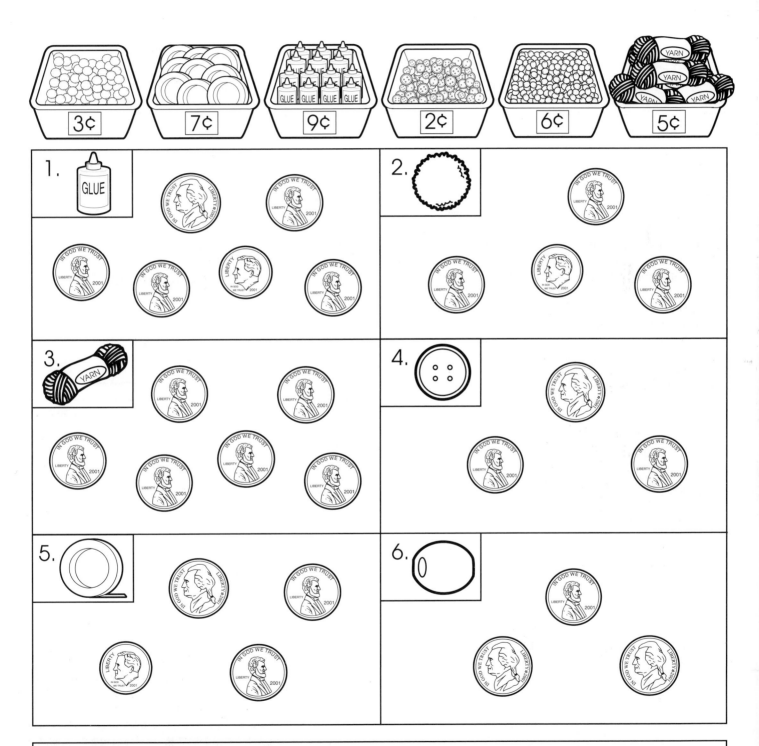

Bonus Box: Choose two of the craft items above. On the back of this sheet, illustrate the two items and write the total cost to buy both.

Identifying fractional parts of a whole

"Quazy" Quilts

Crafty Carl designs quilts with strange patterns.
Look at each quilt.
Write the fraction for each patterned part.

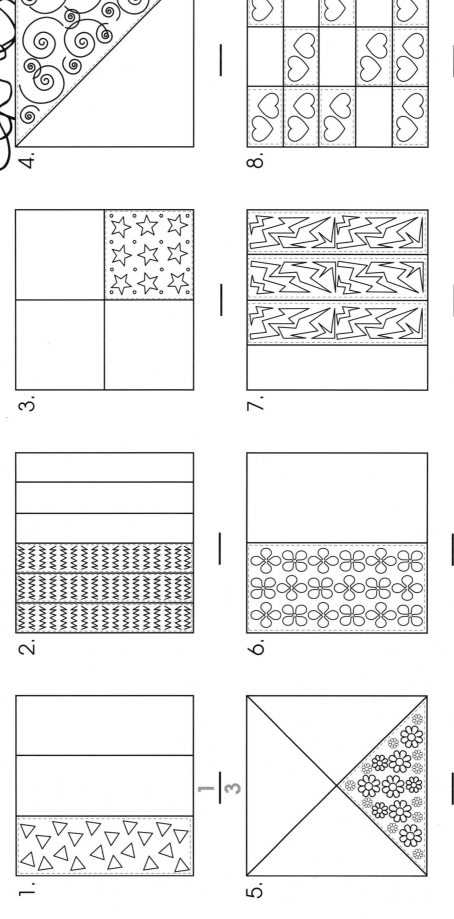

1.

2. ___

3. ___

4. ___

$\dfrac{1}{3}$

5. ___

6. ___

7. ___

8. ___

Bonus Box: On the back of this sheet, draw a quilt design that represents a desired fraction. Write the fraction.

©The Education Center, Inc. • *Out & About Math* • TEC3080 • Key p. 60

Note to the teacher: Use with "Quilt Making" on page 7.

Name_____

Making Time for Fun

Read the calendar.
Read the class schedule.
Cut out each activity box below.
Glue each box in the correct space on the calendar.

Sunday	Monday	Tuesday	Wednesday	Thursday	Friday	Saturday
			1 piano	2 clean room	3	4
5 soccer	6	7	8 piano	9	10	11
12 birthday party	13	14	15 piano	16	17 go to Grandma's	18 soccer
19	20	21 school play	22 piano	23	24	25 soccer
26	27 piano recital	28	29	30	31 slumber party	

Class Schedule
painting: the first and last Monday, Thursday, and Saturday
drawing: the last Wednesday and Sunday
sewing: the second Tuesday and Friday

Answer the questions below.
1. On what day is your first drawing class? _____
2. On what day is your last sewing class? _____
3. How many classes are scheduled for the last week? _____

| painting | painting | painting | drawing | drawing | sewing | sewing |

Out & About at the Pet Store

4 turtles > 2 tarantulas

tarantula 20¢
turtle 50¢
box of crickets 10¢
guinea pig 40¢
frog 30¢

Comparison Shopping

Skills: skip-counting, inequality symbols

Reinforce skip-counting as students compare the prices of popular pet store animals. In advance, cut a pipe cleaner into two two-inch pieces and then lay them beside an overhead projector at the front of the room. Write the pet names and prices shown on the chalkboard. Explain to students that comparing prices when shopping lets them know which item costs less. Using the pipe cleaner pieces, demonstrate how to form each inequality symbol (>, <) and then review how each one is used. Write the names of two different animals and the number of each on the overhead (for example, 4 turtles and 2 tarantulas).

After reading aloud the prices, have a volunteer skip-count by twos to find the total price of the turtles and by fives to find the total price of the tarantulas. Next, have the student form the pipe cleaner pieces into the appropriate inequality symbol and then correctly place it between the animal names *(4 turtles > 2 tarantulas).* Direct him to read the inequality sentence and tell which pet purchase costs less. Continue in this manner with similar examples. If desired, follow up this activity by reading aloud *How Much Is That Guinea Pig in the Window?* by Joanne Rocklin. To provide further practice with skip-counting, have each student complete a copy of "Stocking the Shelves" on page 15. Now that's smart shopping!

Pet Tools		Pet Toys	
brush	20¢	Frisbee toy	10¢
flea collar	20¢	catnip	10¢
food	30¢	scratching post	35¢
treats	15¢	ball	25¢
cage	50¢	yarn	15¢
litter box	30¢	chew toy	20¢
water bottle	20¢	wheel	30¢
food dish	20¢		
pet bed	25¢		

Pet Owner Preparation

Skill: grouping coins

Get students thinking about the amount of money and time needed to provide a new pet with a happy, healthy life. After enlarging the price chart below, copy a class supply of the chart as well as the recording sheet on page 16. Place the copies at a center along with coin manipulatives, crayons, and a pencil. Next, stock your pet center with one of each of the following stuffed animals: a dog, a cat, and a hamster.

As each student visits the center, invite her to choose the pet she would like to buy. Then, on the price list, have the student circle three items needed to properly care for her pet. On a recording sheet, direct her to write the price of each circled item; then have her use the coin manipulatives to find the total cost. Finally, have her complete the rest of the sheet. Once everyone has had an opportunity to visit the center, allow time for students to share their opinions about their findings with the class. To provide further practice with adding coins, have each student complete a copy of "Pet Shopping" on page 17.

Off to the Pet Store

Skills: *making sets, solving word problems*

Help students improve their problem-solving skills with this fun partner game! Ahead of time, create a gameboard similar to the one shown. Then make a copy of the gameboard, as well as the pet cards on page 16, for every two students. If desired, have older students create their own gameboards. Pair students and provide each pair with a set of cards, two game markers, and a supply of manipulatives such as beans or counters. Then direct the pair to cut apart its cards and stack them facedown on a playing surface.

Next, each player places his game marker on Start. Player 1 draws a card, reads it aloud, and offers an answer. If his answer is correct, he moves ahead one space. If his answer is incorrect, he does not move and it becomes Player 2's turn. Encourage players to make sets using the manipulatives to help them answer the questions. Play continues until both players have arrived at Pete's Pet Store. Encourage each player who finishes first to help his partner solve the problems if necessary. Shop til you drop!

Turtle Treats
You have 20 treats.
Your turtle eats 5 each
day.
In how many days
will you run out
of treats?

Legwork

Skills: *skip-counting, making sets*

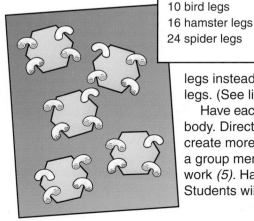

20 turtle legs
10 bird legs
16 hamster legs
24 spider legs

Use this small-group activity to reinforce skip-counting skills. Provide each small group with a supply of pattern blocks, elbow macaroni, and construction paper. Tell students that Mr. Parker, the owner of a local pet store, needs their help taking inventory of the animals in his store. He asked an employee to count each animal, but the employee mistakenly counted each animal's legs instead! For example, instead of counting five turtles, the employee counted 20 turtle legs. (See list above.)

Have each student select a pattern block and place it on her paper to represent one turtle's body. Direct the student to complete the turtle by adding four legs (macaroni). Instruct her to create more turtles so that there are 20 legs all together. Once the group has finished, have a group member share how many turtles Mr. Parker has in his store based on the students' work *(5)*. Have the group continue in this same manner with the remaining animals listed. Students will have a leg up when it comes to making sets!

13

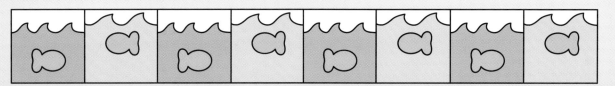

Fancy Fish Patterns
Skill: creating patterns

Foster your students' creativity with this patterning center. In advance, fill a large, clear bowl with goldfish-shaped crackers in three different varieties. Next, create a class supply of 2" x 16" tagboard strips, each divided into eight even sections as shown. Place the bowl of crackers, tagboard strips, a fish net, crayons, and craft glue at a center.

In turn, send each student to the center. Explain that, as a pet store employee, you need to set up the fish tanks in an appealing, patterned display. Tell the students that each tagboard strip represents a display of eight separate fish tanks. Offer suggestions of different ways to form patterns, such as the swimming direction of the fish, the color of the water, the type of fish, the color of the gravel, or the placement of the fish in each tank. After deciding on a pattern, have the student color each tank. Direct him to use the net to "catch" the appropriate fish for each tank and then glue it in place. Replenish the crackers as needed. For an added challenge, have each child continue a classmate's pattern on another strip of paper. What a catch!

Puppy Ponderings
Skill: making a list

collar
ball
leash
shampoo
treats

Try this strategic activity to reinforce students' problem-solving skills. Have each student imagine that she has a puppy that has been awarded first place in the annual dog show. Now the student has to go to the pet store to claim her prizes. Once at the store, she discovers that she has a choice of any two items from the prize list shown above. Before making a decision, the student needs to determine a method to find all of the possible choices. Then, as a class, review the make-a-list strategy.

Next, pair students and provide each pair with five index card halves, a sheet of paper, and a pencil. Have the pair program each card with a different item from the list. Instruct the twosome to use the cards to make a pair to show one combination (for example, a collar and a ball or a collar and a leash). Direct the pair to write its combination on the paper. Have the twosome continue in this manner until all possible combinations have been found. Finally, allow time for each pair to contribute to a class list of the ten possible combinations. If desired, take a class vote to see which prize combination is the favorite!

1. collar, ball
2. collar, leash
3. collar, shampoo
4. collar, treats
5. ball, leash

Name_____

Stocking the Shelves

Study each shelf.
Skip-count to find the total number of
  items on each shelf.

1. Kitty Bites (cans) 3 6 9	Total ____
2. Dog TREATS	Total ____
3. Water	Total ____
4. Pretty Bird MIRROR	Total ____
5. PET Name Tags	Total ____
6. (bones)	Total ____

Bonus Box: Look at the final number of items on each shelf. Circle the odd numbers.
Box the even numbers.

Note to the teacher: Use with "Comparison Shopping" on page 12.

Recording Sheet
Use with "Pet Owner Preparation" on page 12.

Time	Money	
	Item	Cost

Circle your pet.   dog   cat   hamster

✓ yes or no.

Will you walk your pet?   ☐ yes ☐ no   _____   _____

Will you feed your pet?   ☐ yes ☐ no   _____   _____

Will you keep your pet clean?   ☐ yes ☐ no   _____   + _____

Will you play with your pet?   ☐ yes ☐ no   Total

For each ☑ yes add 10 minutes.
How many total minutes are needed for
your pet each day? _____

Pet Cards
Use with "Off to the Pet Store" on page 13.

Kitty Litter	Rabbit Bedding	Bird Seed	Dog Bones
You have 30 cups of litter. You use 10 cups each week. In how many weeks will you run out of litter?	You have 20 cups of bedding. You use 4 cups each week. In how many weeks will you run out of bedding?	You have 3 cups of bird seed. You use 1 cup each week. In how many weeks will you run out of bird seed?	You have 6 bones. Your dog gets 1 bone every other day. In how many days will you run out of bones?
Cheesy Mice Chews You have 15 chews. Your mouse eats 5 a day. In how many days will you run out of chews?	**Kitty Catnip** You have 2 cups of catnip. Your cat gets 1 cup each week. In how many weeks will you run out of catnip?	**Bunny Treats** You have 40 treats. Your bunny gets 10 every other day. In how many days will you run out of treats?	**Cat Food** You have 12 cans of cat food. Your cat eats 1 can each day. In how many days will you run out of cat food?
Turtle Treats You have 20 treats. Your turtle eats 5 each day. In how many days will you run out of treats?	**Pet Vitamins** You have 22 vitamins. Your pet gets 1 each day. In how many days will you run out of vitamins?	**Lizard Snacks** You have 12 snacks. Your lizard eats 4 each week. In how many weeks will you run out of snacks?	**Hamster Snacks** You have 6 snacks. Your hamster eats 2 every other day. In how many days will you run out of snacks?

Pet Shopping

Cut out the coins below.
Lay the fewest coins in each row to
  show each price.
Glue the coins in place.

Pet Shop

Dog Toys ←   Dog Food →

20¢
MY FAVORITE Pet

15¢

50¢

10¢

11¢

5¢

TRAINING YOUR PET
41¢

©The Education Center, Inc. • *Out & About Math* • TEC3080 • Key p. 61

Note to the teacher: Use with "Pet Owner Preparation" on page 12.

Out & About at the Bakery

Baking Measures Up!

Skills: *following directions, selecting appropriate measuring tools*

Strengthen students' measurement skills with this savory whole-class demonstration. In advance, obtain a cake mix and the corresponding ingredients for baking, a can of frosting, different measuring utensils (cups, spoons, rulers, scales), a large bowl, a mixing spoon, and a cupcake pan. Place all of the items on a table at the front of the classroom. Tell each student that as an assistant baker, he must help you bake an order of cupcakes for a customer. Discuss the amount of each ingredient needed and the available measuring tools.

Invite a student volunteer to come forward, select the appropriate measuring tool to measure out one ingredient, and then pour it into the bowl. Repeat this step with different volunteers until each ingredient has been used. Next, stir the batter and then pour the amount indicated in the recipe directions into each muffin cup. After baking the cupcakes and allowing them to cool, decorate them with frosting and enjoy! What a delicious demonstration!

Bakery "Roles"

Skills: *adding coins, making change with coins*

Opening up your own classroom bakery provides endless opportunities to improve math skills. In advance, gather a supply of coins and place each type of coin in a separate storage cup. Label each cup with the corresponding coin name. Then write the price list shown on chart paper. Next, tell students that they will use the coin manipulatives to act out the roles of a baker and a bakery customer.

Invite a pair of students to the center and have each child choose a different role. Have the customer select a total of 50¢ in assorted coins. Instruct him to choose three tasty treats from the list that he can afford. Then have the baker add to find the total cost of the customer's purchase. If desired, provide a calculator to help students with their work. Next, direct the customer to pay for the items with his coins. If necessary, have the baker determine and give the correct change. Instruct the pair to switch roles and repeat the activity. How sweet it is!

Sweet Treats
doughnut 10¢
cupcake 10¢
cookie 5¢
slice of pie 15¢
piece of cake 20¢

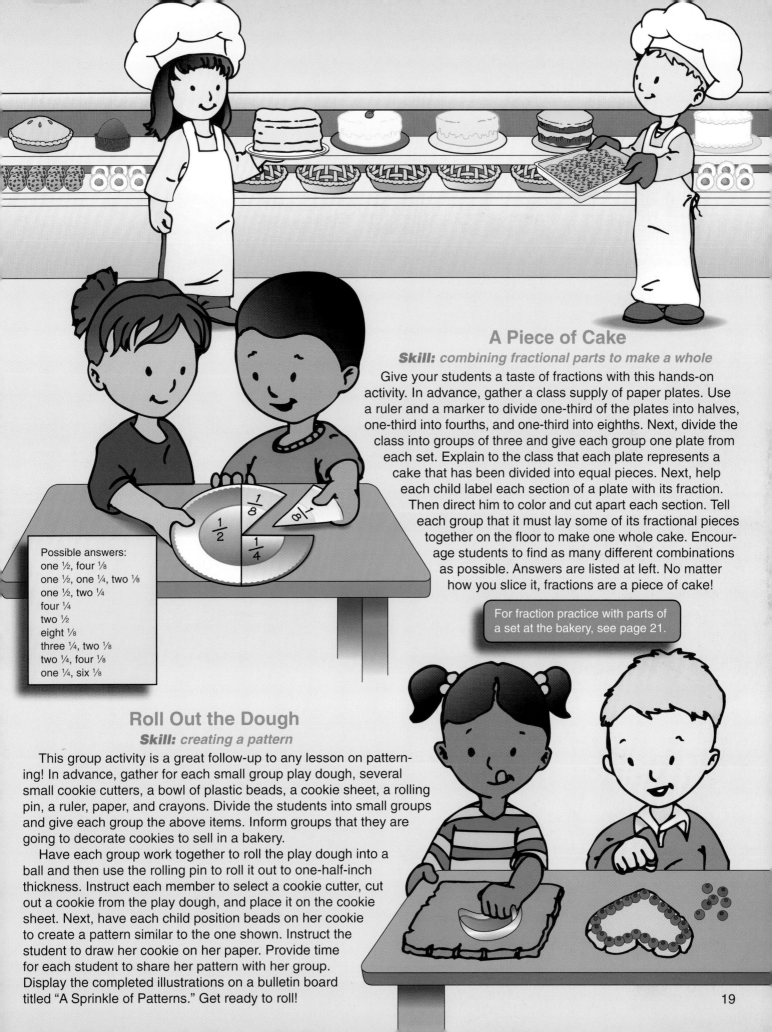

A Piece of Cake

Skill: *combining fractional parts to make a whole*

Give your students a taste of fractions with this hands-on activity. In advance, gather a class supply of paper plates. Use a ruler and a marker to divide one-third of the plates into halves, one-third into fourths, and one-third into eighths. Next, divide the class into groups of three and give each group one plate from each set. Explain to the class that each plate represents a cake that has been divided into equal pieces. Next, help each child label each section of a plate with its fraction. Then direct him to color and cut apart each section. Tell each group that it must lay some of its fractional pieces together on the floor to make one whole cake. Encourage students to find as many different combinations as possible. Answers are listed at left. No matter how you slice it, fractions are a piece of cake!

Possible answers:
one ½, four ⅛
one ½, one ¼, two ⅛
one ½, two ¼
four ¼
two ½
eight ⅛
three ¼, two ⅛
two ¼, four ⅛
one ¼, six ⅛

For fraction practice with parts of a set at the bakery, see page 21.

Roll Out the Dough

Skill: *creating a pattern*

This group activity is a great follow-up to any lesson on patterning! In advance, gather for each small group play dough, several small cookie cutters, a bowl of plastic beads, a cookie sheet, a rolling pin, a ruler, paper, and crayons. Divide the students into small groups and give each group the above items. Inform groups that they are going to decorate cookies to sell in a bakery.

Have each group work together to roll the play dough into a ball and then use the rolling pin to roll it out to one-half-inch thickness. Instruct each member to select a cookie cutter, cut out a cookie from the play dough, and place it on the cookie sheet. Next, have each child position beads on her cookie to create a pattern similar to the one shown. Instruct the student to draw her cookie on her paper. Provide time for each student to share her pattern with her group. Display the completed illustrations on a bulletin board titled "A Sprinkle of Patterns." Get ready to roll!

Solid-Shape Sort

Skills: identifying and sorting solid shapes, graphing

Getting the kitchen organized is simple at this sorting center! Ahead of time, enlist the help of parent volunteers to gather various baking materials, such as clean baking powder cans, baking soda boxes, funnels, rolling pins, and quart-sized milk cartons. Also gather three serving trays or dishpans, labeled as shown, along with a supply of paper. Place the supplies at the center.

Review cones, rectangular prisms, and cylinders with the class. Tell the class that the bakery kitchen is a mess and that each item needs to be put in its proper place. Direct a student to decide on which tray to sort each item according to the item's shape. For example, the funnel is a cone and belongs on the cone tray. Have him continue in this manner until all items have been sorted. To provide further practice with sorting, have each child complete a copy of "Bake Up a Picture Graph" on page 22. Solid shapes are all *sorts* of fun!

Cookie Count

Skill: subtracting

Introduce your students to the wonderful world of baking with this singing activity! Copy the song on the top half of a transparency. Place ten plastic chips on the bottom half of the transparency. Explain to students that the baker at Uptown Bakery is baking cookies to fill an order. However, sometimes he gets very hungry and eats a few. Tell students that their job is to count how many cookies the baker does not eat. Invite a volunteer to come forward as the baker, choose a number from 0 to 10, and then write it on the board. Lead the class in a rendition of the song. Have students use the baker's name and the number she wrote to fill in the blanks while singing. Next, direct her to remove the number of cookies she "ate" to reveal the number of cookies left. Instruct the baker to write the corresponding subtraction sentence on the board. Repeat with a desired number of students. To give students added practice, have each student complete a copy of "Mmm, Mmm, Good Facts" on page 23. Yummy!

Ten Little Cookies
(*sung to the tune of "Ten Little Indians"*)
One little, two little, three little cookies,
Four little, five little, six little cookies,
Seven little, eight little, nine little cookies,
Ten little cookies laying in the pan.
[Student's name] stepped up and ate _____ cookies. (Repeat three times.)
How many cookies are left in the pan?

Cupcake Fun

Read each question.
Write the answer.
Color like cupcakes in each set the same.

1.

a. How many cupcakes in all? _____

b. How many have  ? _____

c. What is the fraction? _____

2.

a. How many cupcakes in all? _____

b. How many have a 🕯 ? _____

c. What is the fraction? _____

3.

a. How many cupcakes in all? _____

b. How many have ? _____

c. What is the fraction? _____

4.

a. How many cupcakes in all? _____

b. How many do not have ? _____

c. What is the fraction? _____

5.

a. How many cupcakes in all? _____

b. How many have ? _____

c. What is the fraction? _____

6.

a. How many cupcakes in all? _____

b. How many have ◎ ? _____

c. What is the fraction? _____

7.

a. How many cupcakes in all? _____

b. How many have ♡ ? _____

c. What is the fraction? _____

8.

a. How many cupcakes in all? _____

b. How many have ☆ ? _____

c. What is the fraction? _____

Bonus Box: On the back of this sheet, draw five cupcakes. Add sprinkles to some of the cupcakes. Write the fraction.

Name _____

Bake Up a Picture Graph

Color and then cut out the pictures at the bottom of the page.
Lay each picture on the row beside its matching shape.
Glue the pictures in place.

Kitchen Duty

Shapes							
cylinder							
rectangular prism							
cone							

Items

Use the graph to answer the questions.

1. How many cylinders are there? _____
2. How many rectangular prisms are there? _____
3. How many cones are there? _____
4. How many more cylinders are there than cones? _____
5. Which shape has the most items? _____

Bonus Box: On the back of this sheet, write one more question about the information on the graph. Then write the answer to the question.

Note to the teacher: Use with "Solid-Shape Sort" on page 20.

Mmm, Mmm, Good Facts

Draw an X on the correct number of cookies.
To complete each number sentence, write
   the missing numbers.
Subtract.

1.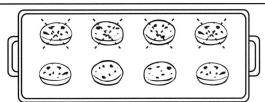

X out 4  .

$$\boxed{8} - \boxed{4} = \boxed{4}$$

2.

X out 6  .

$$\boxed{} - \boxed{} = \boxed{}$$

3.

X out 10  .

$$\boxed{} - \boxed{} = \boxed{}$$

4.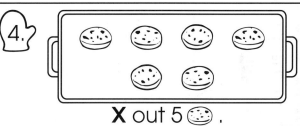

X out 5  .

$$\boxed{} - \boxed{} = \boxed{}$$

5.

X out 3  .

$$\boxed{} - \boxed{} = \boxed{}$$

6.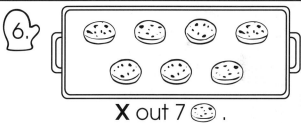

X out 7 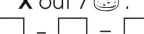 .

$$\boxed{} - \boxed{} = \boxed{}$$

7.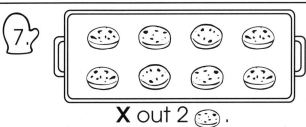

X out 2  .

$$\boxed{} - \boxed{} = \boxed{}$$

8.

X out 9 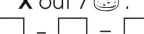 .

$$\boxed{} - \boxed{} = \boxed{}$$

Bonus Box: On the back of this sheet, draw a tray with 9 cookies. Cross out some of the cookies. Write the number sentence to show how many cookies are left.

Note to the teacher: Use with "Cookie Count" on page 20.

Out & About at a Picnic

A Family Picnic
Skill: introducing fact families

Your students are sure to enjoy this hands-on fact-family activity! Tell your class that you need its help packing a picnic basket. Divide students into pairs and give each pair one sheet each of brown, orange, and red construction paper. Instruct the pair to cut out six orange circles (oranges) and six red circles (apples). Next, demonstrate how to pack a given number of real oranges and apples by laying them in a picnic basket. Then state a word problem and instruct each twosome to pack its basket (brown construction paper) with the correct number of oranges and apples. For example, explain that you need to pack six oranges and five apples. Invite a volunteer pair to write an equation on the board showing how many pieces of fruit are in the basket *(6 + 5 = 11)*. Then restate the word problem and have a different volunteer pair write the corresponding fact-family member below the first equation. For example, explain that you put a total of 11 oranges and apples in the basket, but the six oranges rolled out. How many apples are in the basket? *(11 − 6 = 5)* Continue in this manner until the two remaining fact-family members are written on the board *(5 + 6 = 11, 11 − 5 = 6)*. Repeat this process with different fact families as time allows.

Picnic Action
Skill: telling time to the hour and half hour

Any time is picnic time with this creative booklet idea! Have each student stack three 4¼" x 11" sheets of drawing paper and then hold the pages vertically. Instruct her to slide the top sheet upward one inch and the bottom sheet downward one inch. Have the student fold her paper forward to create six graduated layers and then staple the resulting booklet near the fold. Tell each student to write "Time for a Picnic!" on the cover and her name below the title. Write the following incomplete sentence on the board; then direct each student to write it along the bottom of each booklet page: "At _____ : _____ I _____." Next, give each student a copy of the clock patterns on page 27. Have the student cut out and then glue a clock face to the left-hand side of each booklet page. While the glue is drying, explain to students that they need to plan activities for a picnic. Then brainstorm a class list of picnic activities that students have participated in and write the list on the board beside a large, hand-drawn clock face. As you read aloud the incomplete sentence, write a desired time in the space provided. Then have each student write the time in the correct space on her first booklet page as well as a desired activity from the list as shown. Demonstrate how to draw the corresponding clock hands; then have students complete their clocks. Continue in a like manner for each page, allowing students to draw the clock hands on their own. After completing the sentences, encourage students to draw corresponding illustrations on the booklet pages. Once the schedule of activities is complete, have each student complete page 28 for additional practice. Telling time really is a picnic!

A Tisket, a Tasket
Skill: identifying possible outcomes

Help your students explore this probability basket! In advance, put the following number of real apples in a picnic basket: eight red, five green, and two yellow. Review with students the meaning of the word *probability* (the chance or likelihood that an event will happen).

On the board, write how many of each color apple is in your basket and share this information with the class. Ask students which color apple will likely be selected most often if you pull an apple from the basket a number of times equal to the number of your students. Explain that after each apple is pulled, it is returned to the basket. Discuss students' predictions; then have a student remove one apple from the basket without looking. Chart the selection by drawing a tally mark on the board as shown. Then have a student put the apple back in the basket. Repeat this process, using a different student each time. As a class, compare the results with the predictions. If desired, have student pairs make a bar graph to display the findings.

Insect Invasion!
Skills: counting, making sets

Look out! One hundred hungry ants are invading a picnic…your picnic! Prepare your students for some math "ant-ics" with a reading of *One Hundred Hungry Ants* by Elinor J. Pinczes. After reading the story, give each student a copy of the ant patterns on page 27, a resealable plastic bag, a sheet of paper, scissors, and crayons. Discuss with students the variety of insects they have seen on their picnics. Explain that you once set up a picnic too close to a big anthill. There were so many ants, you had trouble counting how many were trying to eat your food. Tell students that you'd like for them to help you find an easy way to group the ants to make counting easier.

Have students cut the ant patterns apart and place them in their bags. Next, have each student count out a desired even number of ants. Then have the student lay her ants in rows, with each row containing an even number. Using crayon dots for the ants, have each student illustrate her work on the provided paper along with a written description of her grouping strategy. Complete this activity several more times using different even numbers. Have older students write a corresponding equation for each illustration. For example, five rows of four ants can be written as "4 + 4 + 4 + 4 + 4 = 20." What a "f-ant-astic" review of counting and grouping objects!

I grouped four ants in each row. There are eight ants all together.

More Hungry Ants

Skills: counting, identifying place value to 100s

Use this center activity to help your students review the counting and grouping of objects. In advance, lay a picnic blanket out at a center. Label each of five index cards with a different letter A through E. Then lay each card on a different paper plate on the blanket in alphabetical order. Next, put a handful of counters (ants)—representing ones, tens, and hundreds—on each plate. Include a supply of paper and pencils at the center. Explain to students that they need to determine which plate has the most ants by counting how many ants are on each plate.

In turn, invite each student to the center to count each set of ants and record his findings. On his paper, have him circle the letter of the plate with the most ants. Then instruct the student to write a sentence about why he would or would not want his food on that plate. Display students' work on a bulletin board titled "An Abundance of Ants!"

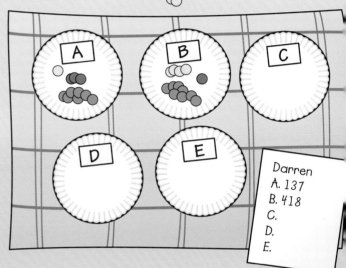

A.	hot dog hot dog	D.	sandwich sandwich
B.	hot dog sandwich	E.	sandwich apple
C.	hot dog apple	F.	apple apple

Chow Time

Skill: making a list

What's a picnic without a few food choices? Encourage students to use the make-a-list strategy to choose which foods they want on their plates. Have your class brainstorm a list of three picnic foods, such as a hot dog, a sandwich, and an apple. Write the list on the board. Then divide the class into pairs. Give each pair a sheet of paper and a pencil. Using the list, instruct the pair to write the two foods it wants on its plate. Students can choose two of one food item. Invite different pairs to share their make-a-list strategies. Write each different combination on the board as it is given. Take a vote to see which combination is the class favorite. Then take your students outside and for an apple-bobbing contest!

Ant Patterns
Use with "Insect Invasion!" on page 25.

Name_____

It's Picnic Time!

Read each sentence below.
Draw the hands on each clock
   to show the correct time.

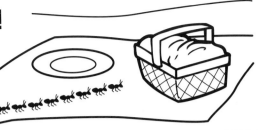

A.  Our picnic begins at 11:00.	B. 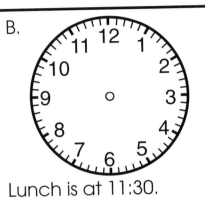 Lunch is at 11:30.	C.  The sack race is one hour after lunch.
D.  The tug-of-war contest is at 1:00.	E.  Dessert is a half hour past 1:00.	F.  We fly a kite a half hour after dessert.
G. 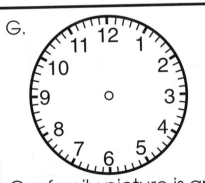 Our family picture is an hour after we fly the kite.	H. The relay race is at 3:30.	I.  Our picnic ends at 4:00.

Bonus Box: Use a red crayon to outline each clock that shows time to the hour.
Use a blue crayon to outline each clock that shows time to the half hour.

©The Education Center, Inc. • *Out & About Math* • TEC3080 • Key p. 61

Finger Food

Read and then cut out the foods below.
List each possible combination of picnic foods.
Use the cards and the key to help you.

KEY
H = hamburger
C = cookie
P = pickle

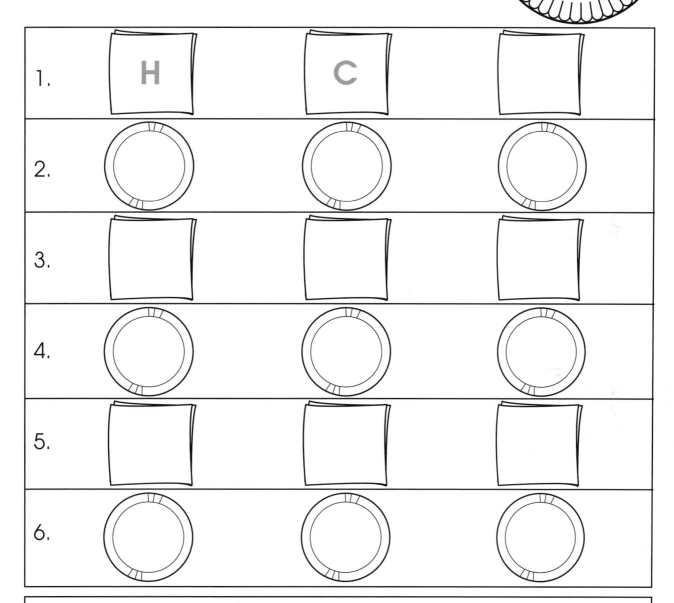

1. H   C

2.

3.

4.

5.

6.

Bonus Box: Mark a picnic food off the list. On the back of this sheet, write two new combinations using the two foods left.

hamburger

cookie

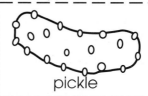

pickle

Note to the teacher: Use with "Chow Time" on page 26.

Birthday Party

It's a Piece of Cake!

Skill: identifying fractional parts of a whole

Any way you slice it, this fraction activity is guaranteed to please! Provide each student with a copy of the cake patterns on page 33. Make an extra copy to cut out and display on an overhead. Have each student carefully cut out his pattern pieces along the heavy solid lines. Next, direct each student to find the circle. Explain that it represents a whole birthday cake. Further explain that the other pieces represent slices of a cake. Begin by asking a student volunteer to come to the overhead and select the pieces that show a cake cut evenly for two people, or in half. Place the pieces beside the whole cake as shown. Direct each student to place his halves atop the circle to show that two halves make a whole. Demonstrate how to write "$\frac{1}{2}$" below the pieces. Emphasize that the cake must be cut into equal-sized pieces in order to accurately represent a fraction. Repeat this process with thirds and fourths. If desired, provide each student with an envelope to store his pieces for later practice with fractions. Students will quickly see that fractions are a piece of cake.

Birthday Bucks

Skill: bill combinations

Challenge students to create a budget for the perfect party and see their math skills really add up. Divide students into groups of three and give each group a sheet of paper, a pencil, and 20 play one-dollar bills. List essential party items—such as decorations, food, and drinks—with your students. Then assign a price to each item, rounded to the nearest dollar. Set a spending limit for the party ($20.00). Next, instruct each group to list on paper the party items it would like to purchase. Have the group write the price beside each item as shown. Direct each group to add the prices and record the total. If the amount is over the set budget, guide the group in making the necessary changes. If desired, provide calculators for groups to check their work. For an added challenge, have each group calculate how much change, if any, it would receive based on the set spending limit. For further practice with adding bills, have each student complete a copy of page 34.

Birthday Budget	
cake	$ 5.00
ice cream	$ 2.00
chips	$ 1.00
soda	$ 2.00
party hats	$ 3.00
party toys	$ 4.00
balloons	$ 2.00
Total	$19.00

Pick a Present
Skill: probability

It's highly probable that your students will enjoy completing this "bow-dacious" activity! In advance, gather five bows of different designs and colors and five sheets of construction paper, each cut to resemble a birthday present. To begin, tape the construction paper presents onto poster board and top each with a bow as shown. Display the poster. Ask students questions about the presents that require them to find the likelihood of choosing a particular present. For example, if three of the presents have bows that are striped, the probability of choosing a present with a striped bow is three out of five. Continue asking similar questions until students begin to understand that probability is the chance or likelihood that an event will happen. To provide further practice with probability, have each student complete a copy of "Grab Bag!" on page 35.

Party Schedule

Play Outdoors
1:00–1:45
Pin the Tail on the Donkey
1:45–2:00
Eat Cake
2:00–2:15
Open Presents
2:15–2:30
Charades
2:30–3:00

Perfect Party Plans
Skills: estimating, making a chart

Fun is on the agenda when you give students the opportunity to create a timetable for their very own party. Create a list of birthday party activities with your students. Include an estimated amount of time each activity will take to complete. Round each time to the nearest half hour or 15 minutes to make scheduling easier. On a sheet of paper, challenge each student to create a chart for a two-hour birthday party schedule similar to the one shown. Encourage organizing the activities in a logical order. Collect the schedules, stack them under a construction paper cover, and staple the pages into a booklet titled "Perfect Party Plans." There's no doubt students will enjoy reading about their classmates' plans for the perfect party.

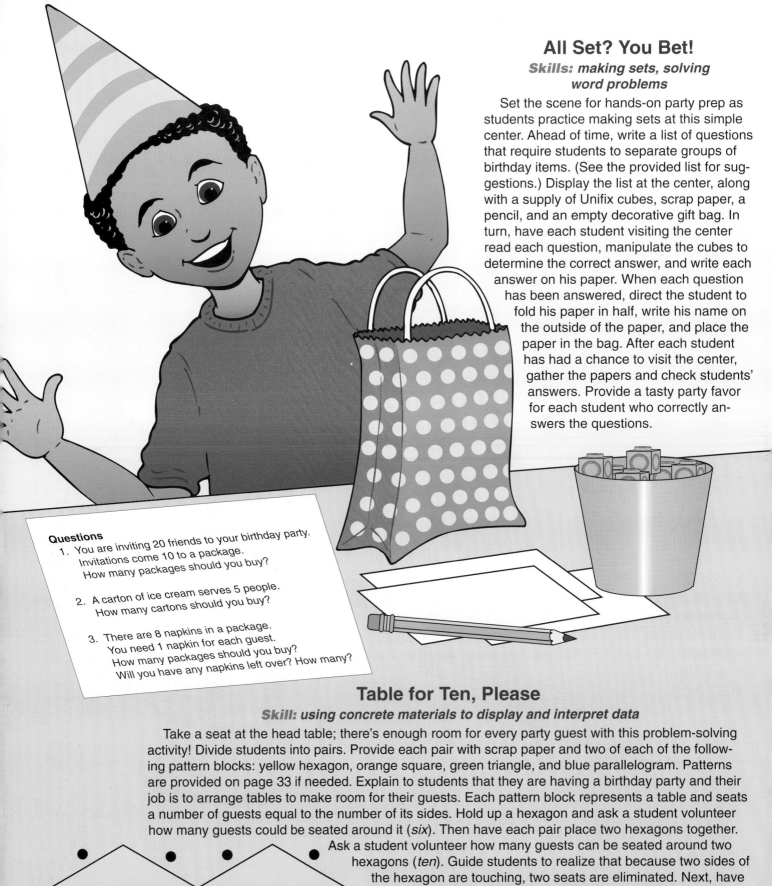

All Set? You Bet!

Skills: *making sets, solving word problems*

Set the scene for hands-on party prep as students practice making sets at this simple center. Ahead of time, write a list of questions that require students to separate groups of birthday items. (See the provided list for suggestions.) Display the list at the center, along with a supply of Unifix cubes, scrap paper, a pencil, and an empty decorative gift bag. In turn, have each student visiting the center read each question, manipulate the cubes to determine the correct answer, and write each answer on his paper. When each question has been answered, direct the student to fold his paper in half, write his name on the outside of the paper, and place the paper in the bag. After each student has had a chance to visit the center, gather the papers and check students' answers. Provide a tasty party favor for each student who correctly answers the questions.

Questions
1. You are inviting 20 friends to your birthday party. Invitations come 10 to a package. How many packages should you buy?

2. A carton of ice cream serves 5 people. How many cartons should you buy?

3. There are 8 napkins in a package. You need 1 napkin for each guest. How many packages should you buy? Will you have any napkins left over? How many?

Table for Ten, Please

Skill: *using concrete materials to display and interpret data*

Take a seat at the head table; there's enough room for every party guest with this problem-solving activity! Divide students into pairs. Provide each pair with scrap paper and two of each of the following pattern blocks: yellow hexagon, orange square, green triangle, and blue parallelogram. Patterns are provided on page 33 if needed. Explain to students that they are having a birthday party and their job is to arrange tables to make room for their guests. Each pattern block represents a table and seats a number of guests equal to the number of its sides. Hold up a hexagon and ask a student volunteer how many guests could be seated around it (*six*). Then have each pair place two hexagons together. Ask a student volunteer how many guests can be seated around two hexagons (*ten*). Guide students to realize that because two sides of the hexagon are touching, two seats are eliminated. Next, have each pair trace the hexagons on paper and color them yellow. Then have the pair place a dot where each guest could sit as shown. Inform students that this combination makes one seating arrangement. Challenge each pair to make other arrangements with any number of pattern blocks to seat ten guests. If desired, check students' answers by drawing the combinations on the board or by using overhead pattern blocks.

ten guests

Use with "Table for Ten, Please" on page 32.

Birthday Budget

Read each price tag below.
Cut out the bills and then lay the correct
  bills in each box.
After completing each row, glue the bills
  in place.

A. $25.00									
B. ICE CREAM ICE CREAM $9.00									
C. FRUIT JUICE FRUIT JUICE $4.00									
D. $7.00									
E. $17.00									

©The Education Center, Inc. • *Out & About Math* • TEC3080 • Key p. 62

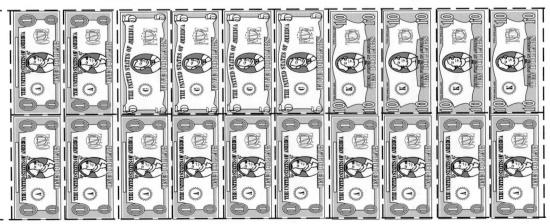

Note to the teacher: Use with "Birthday Bucks" on page 30.

Name _____

Grab Bag!

Color the items in the grab bag.
Use the color code.

Color Code

ring = 1 red, 1 purple
party blower = 1 red, 1 blue
kazoo = 1 green, 1 orange
ball = 1 red, 1 yellow
candy = 1 orange, 1 purple

What is the probability that
you will choose one of the
following items from the bag?
Write your answers on the lines.

- green item

  ____ out of ____

- yellow item

  ____ out of ____

- ring

  ____ out of ____

Probability is the chance
that something will happen.

- red item

  ____ out of ____

- candy

  ____ out of ____

- blue item

  ____ out of ____

- party blower

  ____ out of ____

- orange item

  ____ out of ____

- kazoo

  ____ out of ____

- purple item

  ____ out of ____

Bonus Box: What color item do you think
you would choose most often? Why? Write
your answer in a sentence on the back of
this sheet.

Note to the teacher: Use with "Pick a Present" on page 31.

Bountiful Bouquet
Skill: using tally marks

Enlist your students' help to take inventory of an imaginary flower shop. In advance, draw a tally chart similar to the one shown and then copy to make a class supply. Next, cut out ten simple flower shapes in two different colors. Place the flowers in a lunch bag. Place the bag, the tally charts, and pencils at a center. Explain that a shipment of new flowers has arrived and you need each student to complete a tally chart to determine the flower color of which there is more.

To use the center, have a student shake the bag and, without looking inside, remove one flower. Then have him draw a tally mark beside the corresponding color word. Direct the student to return the flower to the bag and repeat the steps for a total of ten times. Next, tell the student to use the tally marks to help him guess the flower color of which there is more. Have him circle the color word that represents his answer. Then direct him to remove the flowers from the bag, count how many of each color, and check his guess. If the correct answer is different from his own, have him draw a box around the correct color word. To provide additional review of tally marks, have each student complete a copy of page 39. What terrific tally practice!

red	|||
blue	ⵀ ||

Garden of Patterns
Skill: extending a pattern

Watch your students' patterning skills blossom with this fun activity! Label each card in a class supply of index cards with one of the following patterns: "AB," "ABB," or "ABC." Stack and then place the cards in a decorative flowerpot. Explain to each student that as a flower shop employee, she must identify and continue different flower patterns for an outdoor flower garden. Invite a student to the center to select a pattern card and then draw the corresponding flower heads to continue the pattern. Allow the student to choose what kind and color of flowers to draw. Encourage her to repeat the process with different pattern cards as time allows. After each student has had a turn, display the flower patterns near a sign titled "Our Pattern Patch." To provide additional practice, have each student complete a copy of page 40.

Bloomin' Pattern
Skill: *creating a pattern*

Strengthen your students' patterning skills with this hands-on partner activity. In advance, gather potting soil and enough egg cartons for each student pair to have one row of six egg cups. Cut off the lid of each carton and then cut the carton in half lengthwise. Stack and then place the carton sections at a center along with the soil, a ¼-cup measuring cup, a supply of construction paper in six different colors, a supply of craft sticks, scissors, and glue.

To use the center, direct the pair to pour one-fourth of a cup of soil into each of its six egg cups. Next, have the twosome decide on a color pattern for a row of paper flowers (for example, AB, ABB, ABA, or ABC). Have older students create a pattern of a desired flower shape pattern. Tell the partners to cut out and then glue each corresponding flower head to a different craft stick. Then have the pair stick the appropriate flower into each egg cup. For a "living" pattern, have each pair plant different flower seeds in the soil instead of planting the flowers. Explain to students that it will take time for the blooms to appear, so they need to draw the seeds in the order planted to remember the pattern that will grow. What bloomin' good fun!

Flowers for Sale
Skill: *adding two-digit numbers without regrouping*

Your students are sure to enjoy role-playing customers with this partner activity! In advance, make a transparency of the advertisement shown. On the board, write the questions shown below. Pair students and give each pair a set of coin manipulatives. Tell each pair it has a budget of $1.00. Then direct each twosome to use the pricing information and the coins to answer each question. After students have completed the activity, allow time to have different volunteers help answer each question. What savvy consumers!

1. How much does it cost to buy bouquets A and C? Can you buy them? *(73¢; yes)*
2. How much does it cost to buy bouquets B and D? Can you buy them? *(96¢; yes)*
3. How much does it cost to buy 2 of bouquet B and 1 of bouquet C? Can you buy them? *(98¢; yes)*
4. Which bouquets cost more, A and B or D and E? Can you buy them? *(D and E; yes)*

For advanced students:
5. Can you buy 1 of bouquet D and 3 of bouquet A? How much more money do you need? *(no; 41¢)*

A. 23¢

B. 24¢

FOR SALE

C. 50¢

D. 72¢

E. 17¢

©The Education Center, Inc. • *Out & About Math* • TEC3080

Super Strategy
Skill: solving word problems

Use this class activity to strengthen students' problem-solving skills. Create a transparency of the problem shown and display it on an overhead projector. Set a cup of plastic chips beside the overhead. After reading the problem aloud, invite a volunteer to come to the front of the room to solve it. Have him talk through the problem while using the chips to show the class his problem-solving strategy. Repeat this process with a different word problem and a different volunteer. Next, give each student a copy of "Flower Power" on page 41, a resealable bag of manipulatives, and a pencil. After students have completed the page, review it as a class and allow students to share their problem-solving strategies.

[Student's name] bought 6 red flowers, 2 green plants, and 4 purple flowers.
How many flowers did [student's name] buy? *(10 flowers)*

Filling Orders
Skill: reviewing place value to 100s

This hands-on exploration of place value is sure to leave your students feeling quite fulfilled. To set up this center, write each student's last name on a separate index card. Below each name write a different three-digit number (the number of flowers ordered by this person). Stack the cards and then place them at a center along with the following plastic flowers: ten red (hundreds place), ten blue (tens place), and ten yellow (ones place). Next, label three vases as shown. Set the vases at the center near the flowers. Encourage each student to imagine that she is a flower shop employee whose job it is to fill customer orders. Then invite a pair of students to the center. Direct the pair to select one card, read aloud the number of flowers ordered, and then put the correct number of flowers in the corresponding vases. Have the pair empty the vases and repeat the activity with different cards as time allows. Order up!

100s

10s

1s

Mullen
647

Buchholz
121

38

Name _____

Beautiful Bouquet

Color the flowers by the code.
Draw tally marks to complete the chart.

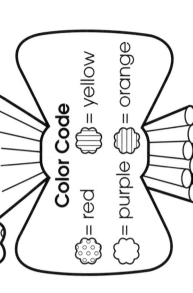

Color Code

 = red   = yellow

= purple   = orange

Color	Tally Marks	Total
red		
yellow		
purple		
orange		

1. Of which color flower is there the most?

2. Draw a picture of the flower of
   which there is the next to least.

3. Of which color flower is there an odd number?

4. Of which two colors are there an equal number?

Note to the teacher: Use with "Bountiful Bouquet" on page 36.

Name_____

Pattern Patch

Read each pattern.
Color each row of flower shop items to match the pattern shown.
Draw and then color the last picture.
Then write the pattern.

 AB

 ABB

 ABC

 **ABBC**

 **ABBA**

Flower Power

Read the story problems.
Write a number sentence to
solve each problem.

A. One daisy has 7 petals.
One daisy has 8 petals.
How many petals in all?

_____ ☐ _____ = _____

B. 12 vases are on a shelf.
7 of them are blue.
How many vases are not blue?

_____ ☐ _____ = _____

C. 8 blooms are purple.
3 blooms are orange.
How many blooms in all?

_____ ☐ _____ = _____

D. You make a bouquet with 11
flowers.
You make one with 6 flowers.
How many flowers in all?

_____ ☐ _____ = _____

E. One flower stem has 10 leaves.
3 leaves wilt and fall off.
How many leaves are left?

_____ ☐ _____ = _____

F. One red rose has 7 thorns.
One yellow rose has 12 thorns.
How many thorns in all?

_____ ☐ _____ = _____

G. Your shop has 30 flowers.
You sell 23 of them.
How many flowers are left?

_____ ☐ _____ = _____

H. One shipment of flowers has
20 daisies.
One has 30 roses.
How many flowers in all?

_____ ☐ _____ = _____

Bonus Box: Choose a word problem from above. On the back
of this sheet, draw a picture to solve it.

Out & About at the Playground

Playground Combinations
Skill: making a list

Use this quick and easy activity to help students get on the move improving their make-a-list skills. Together with students, make a list of playground items and equipment. Divide students into groups of three to five each. Provide each student with an index card. Instruct each group to program each of its cards with a playground item. Then have each group member tape a card to his shirt. Next, have the members in each group work together to maneuver themselves to make as many paired combinations as possible. Have each group list its combinations on paper. Bring the groups together to share their results and strategies with the class. For further practice with making a list, have each student complete a copy of page 45.

teeter-totter/slide
sandbox/swing
sandbox/slide
swing/slide

swing   slide

On Your Mark! Get Set! Go!
Skill: estimating

It's a race against time for students as they exercise their estimation skills with this outdoor activity. To warm up, have each student estimate and record how many times he thinks he can complete a simple task in 15 seconds (for example, writing his name, drawing happy faces, or counting to 25). Time students for 15 seconds as each one completes the activity. Then have each student record the actual number of times he performed the task. Discuss strategies for making more accurate estimations. Then direct each student to make the playground-focused estimation chart as shown. If necessary, adjust the activities and times to match the layout of your school's playground. Next, have each student write an estmate for each activity in red crayon or marker. Grab a stopwatch, and lead students (each with a record sheet and a blue crayon in hand) to the playground. Divide students into four groups. Assign an activity to each group. Set your stopwatch for 15 seconds. On your cue, one member from each group completes the assigned activity. After 15 seconds, have him use a blue crayon to record the actual answer on his chart. Continue in this manner until every student in the group has completed the assigned activity. Rotate the groups until each student has completed all four activities. Lead students back to the classroom to discuss the results. What a workout!

Activity	Time	Estimate	Actual
Slide down the sliding board	15	5	4
Swing forward and back on the swings	15	7	
Swing forward and back on the swings	15	4	
Swing forward and back on the swings	15	3	

Shaping Up the Playground
Skill: identifying plane figures

Your students will see geometry quickly take shape on the playground as they find simple shapes in basic playground equipment. As a class, create a list of common playground equipment. Have students identify a shape within each item. For example, a slide might include a triangle and a rectangle. Lead students to the playground and challenge them to find more shapes within other pieces of equipment. If no playground is available, look at pictures of a playground to search for shapes. Have each child choose one item and instruct him to draw his item on paper using a pencil. Next, have him use a red crayon or marker to color in the shapes found within his item. To complete his drawing, have the student add a sentence as shown. Post the drawings on a bulletin board titled "Shaping Up the Playground."

I see a triangle and rectangles when I look at the sliding board.

The Playground Favorite
Skills: collecting, displaying, and interpreting data

Students will gain valuable experience organizing data as they find out the playground favorite. Provide a copy of page 46 for each student. Instruct each student to fill in the item column with items found on a playground. Next, have each student poll 15 classmates to find out each one's favorite among the listed playground items. If desired, have students venture outside the classroom to poll other children. Direct each student to tally the votes in the tally column. Then instruct each student to count the tally marks and record the total for each item in the total column. Discuss why everyone may not get the same results. *(Students polled different groups of people.)* Finally, have each student create a poster highlighting her winning item.

The Swing Set Was Voted Most Popular With 6 Votes!

All Around the Playground
Skill: identifying spatial relationships

This unique class booklet will get your students thinking about the position of things on the playground. Before beginning the booklet, review positional words with your students, such as *in, on, under, beside,* and *behind.* Then provide each student with a 9" x 6" sheet of white construction paper and access to an ink pad. Assign each child a piece of playground equipment or any item that could be found on a playground. Next, have the student draw her item on the paper. Instruct the child to press her thumb into the ink pad and make a thumbprint on or near the item. Then have her add details to the thumbprint to resemble herself. Direct each student to write a sentence beneath the picture that tells her relationship to the playground item (as shown). Bind all the pages into a booklet titled "All Around the Playground."

I am <u>on</u> the swing.

For Good Measure
Skills: gathering data, nonstandard measurement, graphing

Show students how your playground measures up with this hands-on activity. To begin, discuss with your students that length tells how long an object is and width tells how wide an object is. Also explain that before the invention of the ruler, people sometimes used nonstandard units, such as their fingers, to measure things. For example, the width of four fingers was called a *palm.* Next, have students measure several items in the classroom using their palms. Encourage students to offer observations that explain why different children could measure different lengths for the same object. *(Not all students' palms are the same size.)* Then provide each student with a copy of page 47. As a class, discuss items to be measured on the playground (for example, the width of a swing's seat, the length of a teeter-totter, etc.). Then have each student write the items in the appropriate column on her copy of page 47. Pair students and lead them to the playground. Allow time for each pair to work together to measure each length. Remind each student to use her own palm to measure. Instruct her to record the answer on her paper after each measurement. When all measurements are completed, lead students back to the classroom. Direct students to complete the bar graph for each distance measured. What a great opportunity for students to experience nonstandard measurement firsthand!

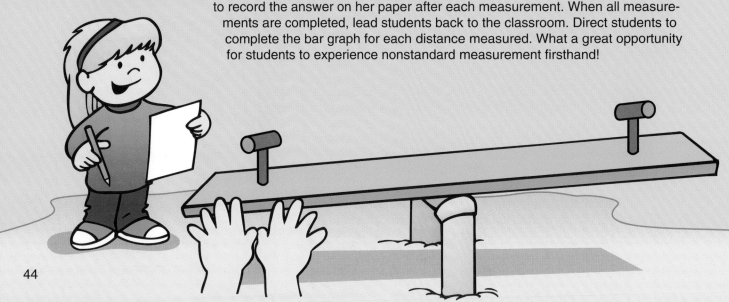

Decisions! Decisions!

Mikey and his friends are at the playground.
Each day, the group of friends can choose only two playground items.
Use the key to list all of their choices on the lines.
Cut out the cards to help you.

Day 1

Key
B = basketball
      hoop
S = slide
J = jungle gym

1. _____
2. _____
3. _____

Day 2

1. _____
2. _____
3. _____
4. _____
5. _____
6. _____

Key
SB = sandbox
B   = ball
SW = swings
M   = merry-go-
         round

©The Education Center, Inc. • *Out & About Math* • TEC3080 • Key p. 63

Note to the teacher: Use with "Playground Combinations" on page 42.

Playground Picks

Ask classmates to vote for their favorite item on the playground.
Mark one tally mark for each person.
Color a circle for each voter until you have asked 15 friends.

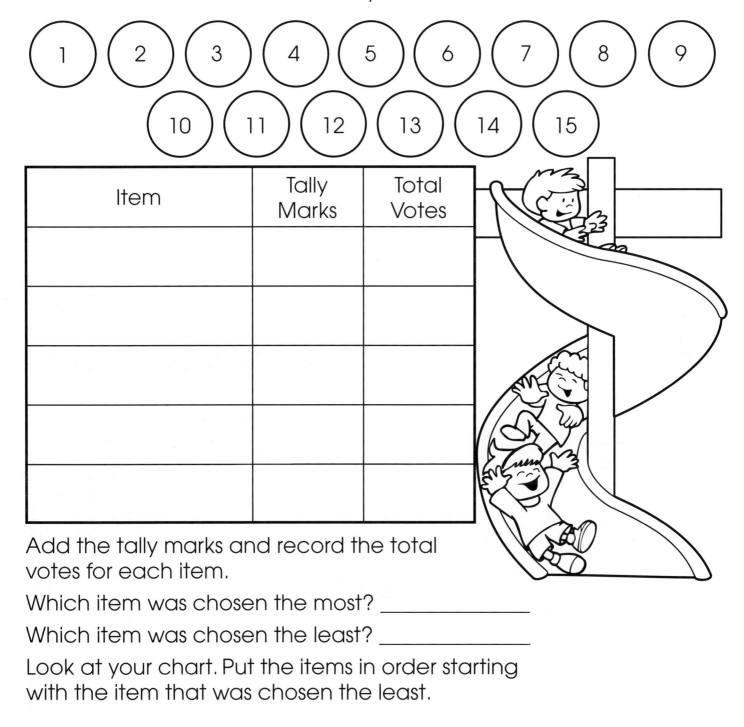

Item	Tally Marks	Total Votes

Add the tally marks and record the total votes for each item.

Which item was chosen the most? _____

Which item was chosen the least? _____

Look at your chart. Put the items in order starting with the item that was chosen the least.

_____

_____

_____

For Good Measure

Think about your playground.
List a playground item on each line.
Measure the distance using your palms.

Item	Palms
1.	
2.	
3.	
4.	
5.	

For each distance measured, color
one box for each palm.

How Many Palms?

Number of Palms					
16					
15					
14					
13					
12					
11					
10					
9					
8					
7					
6					
5					
4					
3					
2					
1					

Items

Bonus Box: Compare your graph to a friend's graph. Write a sentence
on the back of this paper to tell how they are different.

©The Education Center, Inc. • Out & About Math • TEC3080

Note to the teacher: Use with "For Good Measure" on page 44.

Have a Seat!
Skills: making sets, skip-counting

Get ready for a trainload of fun with this hands-on activity! Tell students that a customer visiting their train shop needs a train set with enough passenger cars to seat 50 people. Also share that each train car the shop sells seats four passengers. Next, divide the class into small groups and provide each group with 25 Unifix cubes (each cube represents a train car). Explain to students that they must decide how many train cars are needed to seat the 50 passengers. Lead the groups to count by twos or fours to create the train required *(13 cubes)*.

Next, challenge each group to build a similar train with seating for 70 passengers *(18 cubes)* and then 100 passengers *(25 cubes)*. For older students, assign each color cube a different number of seats (for example, a red cube may have three seats, a yellow cube may have four seats, and a blue cube may have six seats). Then have each group use the cubes to build a train that seats a desired number of passengers. All aboard!

Directions: Use the cubes to build each track. Will the track fit on the shelf? After you build a track, write its name on your paper, draw the track, and answer the question.

one track section = 1 red cube
one bridge = 2 green cubes
one tunnel = 3 yellow cubes

Track Name	Track Parts	Does It Fit?
Canyon Cove Track	2 track sections 2 bridges 1 tunnel	yes
Tall Tree Track	3 track sections 1 bridge 2 tunnels	yes
Rapid River Track	5 track sections 3 bridges 1 tunnel	no
Sunshine Track	5 track sections 1 tunnels	yes

Keeping Track
Skill: measuring length using nonstandard units

Strengthen your students' measuring skills with this center activity. Gather 19 Unifix cubes: five red, six yellow, and eight green. Place the cubes at a center, along with a nine-inch strip of tagboard, paper, and a copy of the directions and chart at the left (without the answers). Explain to students that the tagboard strip is a shelf in the Keep On Trackin' Train Shop. Tell students that they must determine which of four tracks will fit on the shelf.

To use the center, have a student number her paper from 1 to 4. Help her read the directions and the description of Canyon Cove Track. Next, have the student lay the corresponding Unifix cubes on the tagboard strip as shown. Instruct the student to write the name of the track, draw it, and then write "yes" or "no" to tell whether that track will fit on the shelf. Have her continue in this manner with the three remaining tracks. If desired, have each student list the tracks in order from longest to shortest. Now that's keeping track of things!

Tony leaves his house at **7:30** A.M.		
He has to…	**It takes him…**	**The time he finishes is…**
drive to the shop	30 minutes	
collect materials	25 minutes	
put tracks together	45 minutes	
add bridges	20 minutes	
add tunnels	15 minutes	
add decorations	35 minutes	
put trains together	20 minutes	

Race Against the Clock
Skill: *identifying elapsed time*

My, how time flies when students are having fun! Complete this class activity to see whether there's enough time to get the train shop ready to open. Increase the chart shown at left by 200% and then make an overhead transparency. Next, provide each pair of students with a manipulative clock. Display the chart and explain to students that Tony, an employee, has many things to do before the shop opens at 11:00 A.M. As you read aloud an activity, have each pair manipulate its clock to determine at what time Tony finishes that activity. Invite a volunteer to write the answer in the corresponding box on the transparency. Will Tony beat the clock and be able to open the shop on time? Find out! *(Tony will beat the clock.)*

Supplies
boxcars (2, A)
engine cars (3, A)
caboose cars (5, D)
train whistles (5, E)
conductor hats (2, E)
trees (1, D)
bridges (3, E)
tunnels (5, B)
tracks (4, B)
train repair kits (5, A)

In "Training"
Skill: *identifying coordinate points*

Provide practice with coordinate points as students find their way around the train shop! Increase the grid shown by 200% and then make an overhead transparency. Next, program ten index cards, each with a train-set item and its location on the grid (see list). Stack the cards facedown near the chalkboard. Project the grid onto a low section of the chalkboard. Inform students that the grid shows the layout of the shop where they work. Explain to students that it is their first day at work and they must use the grid to learn where each item is located. Also explain that each card includes the name and location of a different train item.

Invite a volunteer to choose a card from the stack and then read it aloud. Instruct her to plot the coordinate points on the grid and then tape the card in place. Have the student explain her plotting strategy. Continue in this manner with other volunteers until every item has been plotted. To provide further practice with plotting coordinate points, have each student complete a copy of "Train Shop Tour" on page 51. Plotting is all in a day's work!

Train Shop

E
D
C
B
A

1 2 3 4 5

Price List

Train car $4.00   Tunnel $2.00   Bridge $3.00

Tree $1.00   Track section $4.00

Train Sets for Sale

Union Atlantic set:
3 Train cars $_____
3 Trees $_____
4 Track sections $_____
Total cost $_____ ($31.00)

Southeastern set:
2 Train cars $_____
1 Tree $_____
1 Tunnel $_____
2 Track sections $_____
Total cost $_____ ($19.00)

Western Express set:
2 Train cars $_____
5 Track sections $_____
2 Bridges $_____
Total cost $_____ ($34.00)

A & B Steam set:
4 Train cars $_____
1 Tunnel $_____
2 Track sections $_____
1 Bridge $_____
Total cost $_____ ($29.00)

Trains for Sale
Skill: adding bills

How much is that train in the window? Help your students find the answer while strengthening their addition skills. In advance, write the price list and the train-set list shown above on the chalkboard (without the italicized answers). Pair students and provide each pair with a calculator. Explain that each pair has a $20 budget with which to shop for a toy train set.

To determine which set it can buy, have the pair use both lists and the calculator to calculate each set's total cost. Then direct each pair to write each set's name and total cost on paper. Call on volunteers to write the total cost in the corresponding blanks on the board. Have the class state which set it can buy *(Southeastern set)*. If desired, have students order the sets from least to most expensive. For further practice with adding money, have each student complete a copy of "Model Math" on page 52.

Create-a-Train
Skills: recognizing even and odd numbers, skip-counting

Build your students' skip-counting skills with this fun activity. Provide each student with a copy of page 53, two 12-inch sentence strips, scissors, crayons, and glue. Have each student imagine that as an employee of a train shop, she has received two new train sets from The Boxcar Train Company. Explain that the trains are in pieces and must be put together. The two trains in the sets are the Odd Number train and the Even Number train.

Direct each student to cut out the train patterns. Then have her separate the odd-numbered cars from the even-numbered cars into two sets. Next, have the student place the odd-numbered cars in ascending order to make the Odd Number train. Have her glue the cars in order on one sentence strip and then label the train as shown. Have her make the Even Number train in the same manner on the other sentence strip. Allow time for students to decorate their trains. Toot! Toot!

Train Shop Tour

It's your first visit to the train shop.
Study the map.
Use the map to answer the
    questions below.

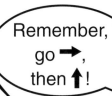

Remember,
go ➡,
then ⬆!

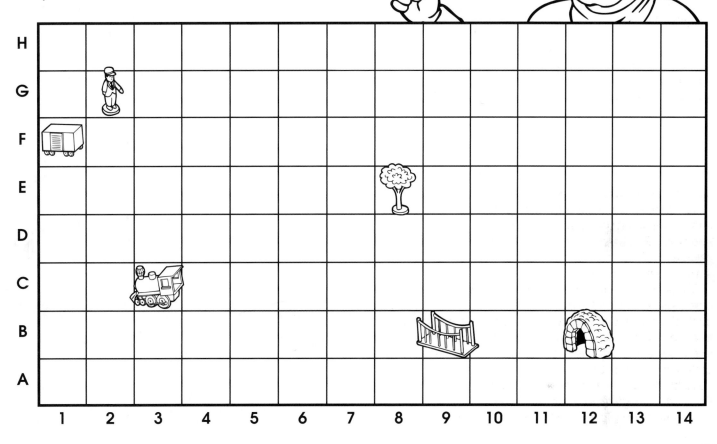

1. Which item will you find at (8, E)? _____

2. Write the location of the conductor. _____

3. Write the location of the tunnel. _____

4. Which item will you find at (3, C)? _____

5. The train whistles are at (6, D). Draw a 🎇 there.

6. Which item will you find at (1, F)? _____

7. Write the location of the bridge. _____

8. The tracks are at (12, G). Draw a 🛤 there.

Bonus Box: Draw a 🚃 on the map. Then write its location on the line. _____

Note to the teacher: Use after completing "In 'Training' " on page 49.

Model Math

Look at the model train set below.
Find the total cost of each item.
Find the total cost of the set. Write it in the space provided.

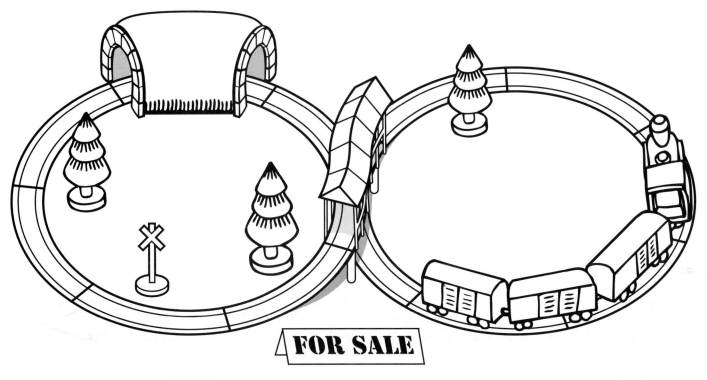

FOR SALE

Item	How many?	Cost Per Item	Total Cost
Track Section	13	$1.00	
Train Engine		$5.00	
Boxcar		$1.00	
Tree		$1.00	
Sign		$2.00	
Bridge		$3.00	
Tunnel		$3.00	

Total Cost of Set _____

Bonus Box: You got $30.00 for your birthday. Can you buy the train set above? How much more money do you need?

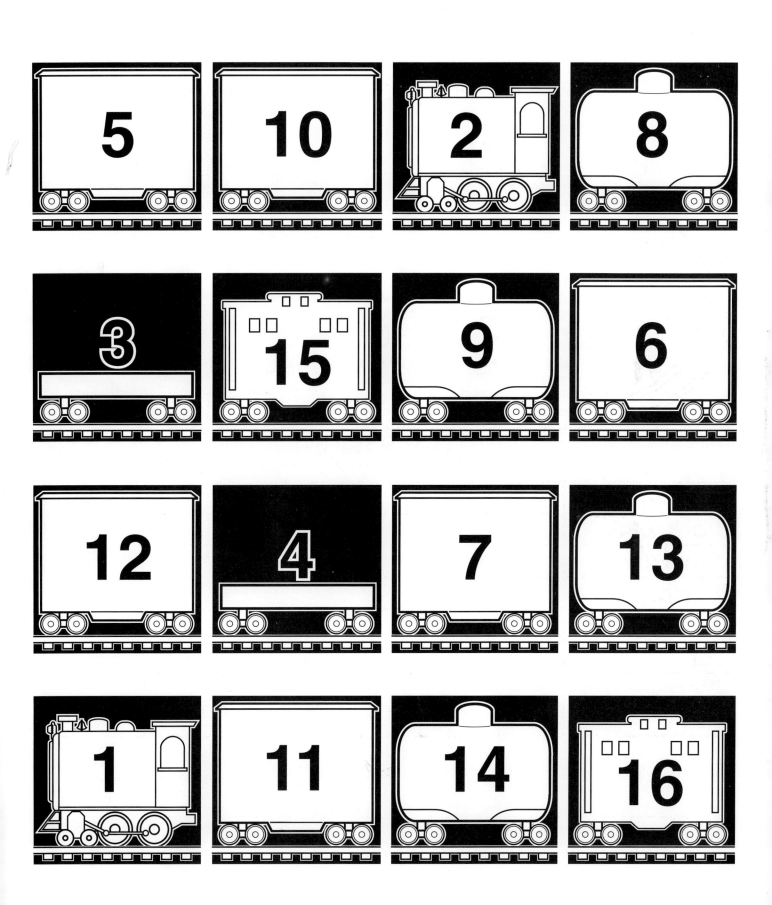

Out & About at the Post Office

Order in a Zip
Skill: ordinal numbers

Use this activity to show your students that even mail has a special order! Ahead of time, address each of five envelopes with a different house number from 12 to 16. Then shuffle the envelopes and lay them on the chalkboard ledge at the front of the room. Label five empty containers with the following street information: "Street 12," "Street 13," "Street 14," "Street 15," and "Street 16." Explain to students that you need their help sorting the mail by house number into the correct bins.

Have a volunteer come to the front of the room and select an envelope, read the house number, and then lay the envelope in the correct bin. Repeat this step with different volunteers until each envelope is in its correct bin. Next, ask questions that prompt students to think about which envelope will be delivered third, fifth, second, fourth, and first. Encourage students to talk with a partner to determine the answers. Discuss the correct answers as a class. Now that's an activity with a lot of zip!

Lengthy Measures
Skill: measuring length using standard units

This hands-on center activity is sure to strengthen your students' measurement skills! In advance, draw an envelope design on six 3" x 5" index cards, two 4" x 6" index cards, and four 5" x 7" index cards. Shuffle the cards and lay them in a stack at a center. Make a class supply of the graph on page 57 and place the graphs at the center along with a supply of paper, rulers, and crayons. Display the questions shown at the center for students to answer. Explain to students that they must reorder envelopes for their post office when an envelope's count is down to five or fewer. To use the center, a student selects one envelope from the stack, measure it in inches using a ruler, and then shades the corresponding box on the graph. Direct the student to continue this process with each envelope and then to use the graph to answer the related questions.

1. Of which envelope do you have the most? *(3" x 5")*
2. Of which envelope do you have the least? *(4" x 6")*
3. How many more 3" x 5" envelopes are there than 4" x 6"? *(four more)*
4. Which envelopes do you need to restock? *(4" x 6" and 5" x 7")*

Vending Machine Values
Skill: adding

Reinforce your students' addition skills with this great postal activity. Make a class supply of the reproducible on page 58. Place the copies at a center along with coin manipulatives and pencils. To introduce the center, tell students that their parents have sent them to the post office to buy certain stamps. Explain that if they need to buy a stamp and the main desk is closed or it's too busy for them to wait in line, they can use the stamp vending machine in the lobby. Tell them that it works a lot like a drink machine, in that they look for what they need, read the price, put that amount of money into the machine, and then press the correct button. Then their stamps come out of the machine for them to use. At the center, have a volunteer look at the vending machine stamps and their prices. Then have her read each list of stamps to buy. Instruct her to write each stamp's price and then use the coins to help add how much money she needs. What super stamp fun!

Stamp of Approval
Skills: using tally marks, conducting a survey

It's time to vote on a new stamp! In advance, create three stamp designs on the provided recording sheet on page 57; then make a class supply. Enlarge and then display one set of the stamps at the front of the classroom. Explain to students that the post office often comes out with a new stamp after voting on several choices. Tell students that they are going to conduct a survey using tally marks to see which stamp is the overall favorite. Discuss each stamp design. Then give a copy of the recording sheet to each student. Instruct the student to ask ten people at recess (or at a time when your students are around other classes) which stamp is their favorite and to mark each person's choice on the recording sheet with a tally mark. After your students return to class, compile the results into a class recording sheet on the board. Discuss the findings; then take a class vote and compare the results to the survey findings.

Express Delivery

Skills: *reading a calendar, completing a chart*

Have your students ever wanted to mail something and have it reach its destination the very next day? Use this activity to review completing a chart using a calendar. Make a class supply of the reproducible on page 59. Give each student a copy, along with a pencil, scissors, and glue. Discuss with students the following common types of mail delivery: express (about one day), priority (about three days), and first class (about eight days, depending on how far it has to travel). Help students read the directions and complete the calendar and the chart to determine mail delivery dates. Then divide the class into pairs and allow partners to discuss their work. Now that's a first-class activity!

Weighing In

Skills: *using a balance, estimating and comparing, using inequality and equality symbols*

Try this whole-class activity to review measurement of weight. In advance, fill five boxes of varying sizes with different materials that add weight, such as beans, sand, and Unifix cubes. Seal the boxes and wrap each in brown paper. Then gather a balance scale, a small box of crayons wrapped in brown paper to use as the constant weight, three cards marked with different symbols (<, =, and >), and two storage trays. Explain to students that, as postal employees, they must sort packages by weight into two different trays for shipping. The lighter packages go in one tray, and the heavier packages go in the other tray.

Display the balance at the front of the classroom. Lay the constant weight in the right pan and one of the lighter packages in the left pan. Ask students which object is lighter. Ask a volunteer to explain how he determined his answer. *(The left pan moved up, so that object is lighter. The pan with the heavier object moved down.)* Have the volunteer place the correct symbol on the table between the two objects (<). Then have him place the object in the tray for lighter packages. Continue in this manner with the remaining objects and different volunteers. After all objects are weighed, ask students which tray has the greater number of objects. Then ask students how their answers might change if they used a lighter constant. "Weigh" to go!

Mighty Measurement

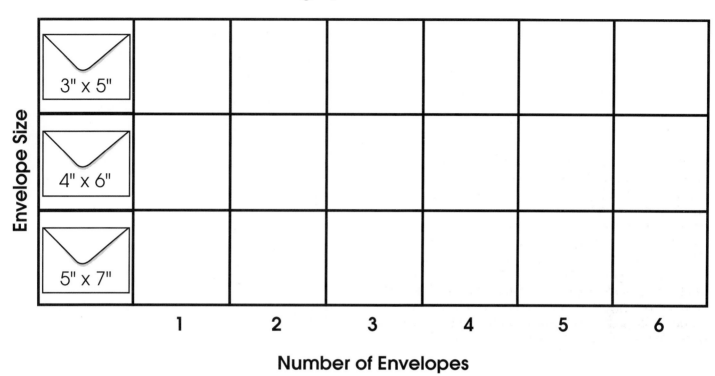

Envelope Size

| | 3" x 5" | 4" x 6" | 5" x 7" |

1   2   3   4   5   6

Number of Envelopes

Ask 10 people which stamp is their favorite. Draw a tally mark for each response.		Total

Stamp Sense

Follow your teacher's directions.

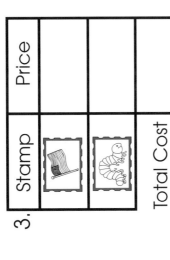

1¢ =	10¢ =
5¢ =	25¢ =

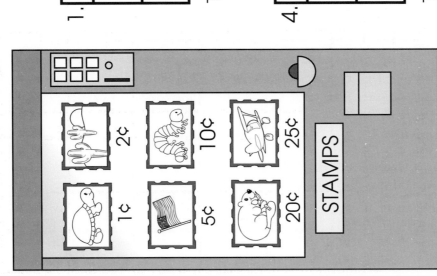

1. Stamp	Price
	2¢
	1¢
Total Cost	3¢

2. Stamp	Price
Total Cost	

3. Stamp	Price
Total Cost	

4. Stamp	Price
Total Cost	

5. Stamp	Price
Total Cost	

6. Stamp	Price
Total Cost	

Bonus Box: Choose three different stamps from the machine. On the back of this paper, draw the stamps and then add their total cost.

©The Education Center, Inc. • *Out & About Math* • TEC3080 • Key p. 63

Note to the teacher: Use with "Vending Machine Values" on page 55.

Name _____

It's in the Mail

Study the delivery schedule and the mailing chart
for Dottie's Delivery Service.
Cut out the labels at the bottom of the page.
Lay each label in the correct box on the calendar.
Glue the labels in place.

Delivery Schedule

Express ....1 day
Priority ....3 days
First Class ....8 days

Date Mailed	Type	Arrival Date
A. March 7	Priority	March 10
B. March 15	Express	
C. March 23	First Class	
D. March 1	First Class	
E. March 11	Priority	
F. March 20	Express	
G. March 17	Priority	
H. March 21	First Class	

MARCH

Sunday	Monday	Tuesday	Wednesday	Thursday	Friday	Saturday
			1	2	3	4
5	6	7	8	9	10	11
12	13	14	15	16	17	18
19	20	21	22	23	24	25
26	27	28	29	30	31	

FC   FC   FC   P   P   P   E   E   E

©The Education Center, Inc. • *Out & About Math* • TEC3080 • Key p. 63

Note to the teacher: Use with "Express Delivery" on page 56.

Answer Keys

Page 9

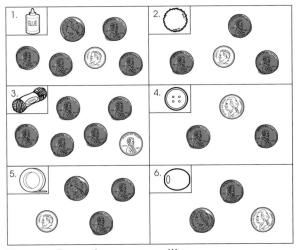

Bonus Box: Answers will vary.

Page 10

1. ⅓
2. ³⁄₆ or ½
3. ¼
4. ½
5. ¼
6. ½
7. ¾
8. ¹⁰⁄₁₅ or ⅔

Bonus Box: Answers will vary.

Page 11

Sunday	Monday	Tuesday	Wednesday	Thursday	Friday	Saturday
			1 piano	2 clean room	3	4 painting
5 soccer	6 painting	7	8 piano	9	10	11
12 birthday party	13	14 sewing	15 piano	16	17 go to Grandma's	18 soccer
19	20	21 school play	22 piano	23	24	25 soccer
26 drawing	27 piano recital	28	29 drawing	30 painting	31 slumber party	

1. Sunday, the 26th
2. Tuesday, the 14th
3. 3

Page 16

Kitty Litter: 3 weeks
Rabbit Bedding: 5 weeks
Bird Seed: 3 weeks
Dog Bones: 11 days
Cheesy Mice Chews: 3 days
Kitty Catnip: 2 weeks
Bunny Treats: 7 days
Cat Food: 12 days
Turtle Treats: 4 days
Pet Vitamins: 22 days
Lizard Snacks: 3 weeks
Hamster Snacks: 5 days

Page 15

1. 21
2. 24
3. 12
4. 35
5. 50
6. 32

Bonus Box: circled—21, 35; boxed—24, 12, 50, 32

Page 17

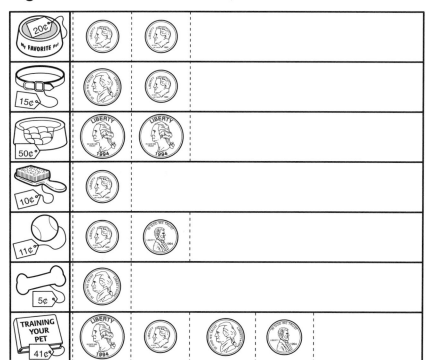

Page 23

1. $8 - 4 = 4$
2. $12 - 6 = 6$
3. $15 - 10 = 5$
4. $6 - 5 = 1$
5. $11 - 3 = 8$
6. $7 - 7 = 0$
7. $8 - 2 = 6$
8. $10 - 9 = 1$

Bonus Box: Answers will vary.

Page 28

A. 11:00, red
B. 11:30, blue
C. 12:30, blue
D. 1:00, red
E. 1:30, blue
F. 2:00, red
G. 3:00, red
H. 3:30, blue
I. 4:00, red

Bonus Box: Each clock should be outlined in the color indicated above.

Page 21

1. a. 3
    b. 1
    c. $\frac{1}{3}$
2. a. 4
    b. 2
    c. $\frac{2}{4}$ or $\frac{1}{2}$
3. a. 2
    b. 1
    c. $\frac{1}{2}$
4. a. 6
    b. 5
    c. $\frac{5}{6}$

5. a. 6
    b. 3
    c. $\frac{3}{6}$ or $\frac{1}{2}$
6. a. 3
    b. 2
    c. $\frac{2}{3}$
7. a. 4
    b. 3
    c. $\frac{3}{4}$
8. a. 8
    b. 4
    c. $\frac{4}{8}$ or $\frac{1}{2}$

Bonus Box: Answers will vary.

Page 22

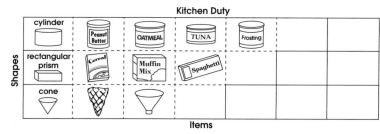

1. 4
2. 3
3. 2
4. 2
5. cylinder

Bonus Box: Answers will vary.

Page 29

Order of answers may vary.

1. HCP
2. HPC
3. CPH
4. CHP
5. PHC
6. PCH

Bonus Box: Answers will vary.

Page 34

A. $25.00	$10.00	$10.00	$5.00						
B. $9.00	$5.00	$1.00	$1.00	$1.00	$1.00				
C. $4.00	$1.00	$1.00	$1.00	$1.00					
D. $7.00	$5.00	$1.00	$1.00						
E. $17.00	$10.00	$5.00	$1.00	$1.00					

Page 35

green item	1 out of 10
yellow item	1 out of 10
ring	2 out of 10
red item	3 out of 10
candy	2 out of 10
blue item	1 out of 10
party blower	2 out of 10
orange item	2 out of 10
kazoo	2 out of 10
purple item	2 out of 10

Bonus Box: Red. More items are red than any other color.

Page 39

Color	Tally Marks	Total
red	IIII I	6
yellow	IIII II	7
purple	IIII IIII	10
orange	IIII I	6

1. purple
2.
3. yellow
4. red and orange

Page 41

A. $7 + 8 = 15$
B. $12 - 7 = 5$
C. $8 + 3 = 11$
D. $11 + 6 = 17$
E. $10 - 3 = 7$
F. $7 + 12 = 19$
G. $30 - 23 = 7$
H. $20 + 30 = 50$

Bonus Box: Answers will vary.

Page 45

Order of answers may vary.

Day 1
1. B—S
2. B—J
3. S—J

Day 2
1. SB—B
2. SB—SW
3. SB—M
4. B—SW
5. B—M
6. SW—M

Page 51

1. tree
2. (2, G)
3. (12, B)
4. engine
5. train whistle at (6, D)
6. boxcar
7. (9, B)
8. track at (12, G)

Bonus Box: Answers will vary.

Page 52

Item	How Many?	Cost Per Item	Total Cost
Track Section	13	$1.00	$13.00
Train Engine	1	$5.00	$5.00
Boxcar	3	$1.00	$3.00
Tree	3	$1.00	$3.00
Sign	1	$2.00	$2.00
Bridge	1	$3.00	$3.00
Tunnel	1	$3.00	$3.00

Total Cost of Set $32.00

Bonus Box: No, $2.00.

Page 58

1. 2¢
   1¢
   3¢

2. 5¢
   2¢
   7¢

3. 5¢
   10¢
   15¢

4. 20¢
   20¢
   40¢

5. 20¢
   10¢
   30¢

6. 25¢
   1¢
   26¢

Bonus Box: Answers will vary.

Page 59

A. March 10
B. March 16
C. March 31
D. March 9
E. March 14
F. March 21
G. March 20
H. March 29

Managing Editor: Deborah G. Swider

Editor at Large: Diane Badden

Staff Editor: Kelly Coder

Contributing Writers: Lisa Buchholz, Vicki Dabrowka, Julie Hayes, Starin Lewis

Copy Editors: Sylvan Allen, Karen Brewer Grossman, Karen L. Huffman, Amy Kirtley-Hill, Debbie Shoffner

Cover Artists: Nick Greenwood, Clint Moore

Art Coordinator: Nick Greenwood

Artists: Pam Crane, Theresa Lewis Goode, Nick Greenwood, Clevell Harris, Ivy L. Koonce, Sheila Krill, Clint Moore, Greg D. Rieves, Rebecca Saunders, Barry Slate, Donna K. Teal

Typesetters: Lynette Dickerson, Mark Rainey

President, The Mailbox Book Company™: Joseph C. Bucci

Director of Book Planning and Development: Chris Poindexter

Book Development Managers: Cayce Guiliano, Elizabeth Lindsay, Thad McLaurin, Susan Walker

Curriculum Director: Karen P. Shelton

Traffic Manager: Lisa K. Pitts

Librarian: Dorothy C. McKinney

Editorial and Freelance Management: Karen A. Brudnak

Editorial Training: Irving P. Crump

Editorial Assistants: Hope Rodgers, Jan E. Witcher

www.themailbox.com

©2003 by THE EDUCATION CENTER, INC.
All rights reserved.
ISBN# 1-56234-525-7

Manufactured in the United States
10 9 8 7 6 5 4 3 2 1